Led to Lead

A 28 Day Devotional on Christian Leadership

Led to Lead

A 28 Day Devotional on Christian Leadership

By Donald C. Benson, Jr.

Published by Love, Sharing, Faith Ministry

Copyright © Donald C. Benson, Jr 2025

All rights reserved. No part of this publication may be reproduced, stored in a retrieval system, or transmitted, in any form or by any means, electronic, mechanical, photocopying, recording or otherwise, without the prior permission of the publishers.

The author has made every effort to ensure the accuracy of the information within this book was correct at time of publication.

For requests, information, and more contact Donald C. Benson, Jr at lovesharingfaith@outlook.com

Table of Contents

My Testimony 1

Introduction 7

   Day 1: Called to Lead 9

   Day 2: The Heart of a Shepherd 12

   Day 3: Servant Leadership 16

   Day 4: Leading with Vision 20

   Day 5: Faith Over Fear 24

   Day 6: Leading Through Trials 28

   Day 7: Guarding Your Heart 32

   Day 8: Leading with Wisdom 36

   Day 9: Leadership and Courage 40

   Day 10: Leading with Integrity 44

   Day 11: Leading by Example 48

   Day 12: The Power of Prayer in Leadership 52

   Day 13: Leading with Compassion 56

   Day 14: Leadership and Accountability 60

   Day 15: Leading with Patience 64

Day 16: Leading with Humility 68

Day 17: Discernment in Leadership 72

Day 18: Leading in Love 76

Day 19: Vision and Clarity 80

Day 20: Leading with Endurance 84

Day 21: Leading in Truth 88

Day 22: Leading Through Change 92

Day 23: Leading with Joy 96

Day 24: The Power of Encouragement 100

Day 25: Humility in Leadership 104

Day 26: The Cost of Leadership 108

Day 27: Finishing Strong 112

Day 28: The Legacy of Leadership 116

Conclusion 120

My Testimony

God has been so good to me. Yet, like every believer, my journey has been marked by both blessing and brokenness—by moments of deep loss and divine restoration. I was born and raised in a small community in northeastern Virginia, the son of loving, hard-working, middle-class parents. My mother stayed at home to raise my sister and me, while my father served faithfully as a police officer in Lancaster County.

Everything changed on November 5, 1981. I was only five years old when my father was killed in the line of duty. In a single moment, I lost the man who was my protector and my example. Though I was too young to remember much about him, that day forever altered the course of my life.

But even in tragedy, God provided. My mother, through grace and strength that could only come from the Lord, raised us with faith and perseverance. Our church family at Claybrook Baptist Church in Weems, Virginia surrounded us with love and compassion. I was never without care or encouragement. Though my earthly father was gone, my heavenly Father was already writing a story of faithfulness.

As I grew older, however, questions began to take root in my heart. I wrestled with the age-old questions many have asked: *Why would a loving God allow such pain? Why did He take my father? What had I done to deserve this loss?* These thoughts followed me into adulthood, especially during my college years at Radford University. I searched for a church home but never found one that felt right. Gradually, I drifted from the Lord. My faith weakened, my prayers faded, and my focus turned inward.

But here's the beautiful truth about God—He never stops pursuing His children. Even when we wander, He remains faithful.

During that season of rebellion, I surrounded myself with the wrong influences. I began to drink, smoke, and live for pleasure rather than purpose. Eventually, I met and married a woman who did not share my faith. I convinced myself it didn't matter—but deep down, I knew it did. Over time, the distance between us grew, and when she eventually told me she no longer loved me, my world collapsed.

I found myself broken, living on the couch of two dear friends—Chris and Heather Weeks—who became instruments of God's grace. They showed me love when I couldn't love myself. Yet even with their care, darkness lingered in my heart. I felt empty, worthless, and without hope. I no longer wanted to live.

And then God intervened.

One morning, driving to work, I connected my new phone to the car radio. Out of nowhere, a song I hadn't heard in years began to play—*"Jesus, Take the Wheel"* by Carrie Underwood. As those words filled the car, I felt the presence of God in that moment. I had to pull over, weeping as the Holy Spirit broke through years of hardness and pride. For the first time in over fifteen years, I prayed. In that moment, God reminded me that He had never left me. That song was not random—it was redemption.

Not long after, God brought Heather into my life—the woman who would become my wife and my greatest earthly blessing. Through her love and faith, I found my way back to the Lord. My heart was renewed, and I finally surrendered to the calling I had resisted for so long. I had always loved teaching, but God revealed that my true calling was not only to teach—but to *preach*.

Today, I serve as a minister, evangelist, and teacher of the Gospel. God led me to launch a ministry called **Love, Sharing, Faith**, dedicated to "real talk about real Gospel for real life." Through devotionals, sermons, and multimedia outreach, I have seen God open doors to reach people far beyond what I ever imagined.

Yet the story doesn't end there.

Heather and I always knew that God's plan for our lives included children. Though we tried for years to conceive, we were never able to. After much prayer, God redirected our hearts toward foster care—a journey that would test our faith and reveal His miraculous power.

In 2021, we received a call about a little girl named Bryn. She had endured unimaginable suffering—born at 26 weeks, losing her mother to a brain aneurysm, and later surviving horrific abuse that left her with severe injuries. Doctors said she wouldn't live through the day. But God had another plan. He restored her hearing completely, her sight in one eye, and gave her the strength to stand and walk with assistance. Though Bryn still battles the effects of cerebral palsy and shaken baby syndrome, she radiates joy, courage, and the unbreakable spirit of one who has been touched by the hand of God. Bryn is one of the most loving and caring children I have ever met and she loves to sing and praise the Lord.

In January 2024, God completed what He had begun—we adopted Bryn as our daughter. She is a daily reminder that God brings beauty from ashes and purpose from pain.

Through every trial and every triumph, God has proven Himself faithful. I have learned to thank Him not only for the blessings but for the storms that shaped me. Every loss, every question, and every moment of brokenness was part of His divine plan to bring me to where I am today.

I stand here as living proof that no one is too far gone, no story too broken, and no past too painful for God to redeem. My life is a testimony to His mercy, His patience, and His unshakable grace. God is GREAT!

INTRODUCTION

Leadership in today's world often revolves around power, prestige, and personal ambition. Titles and influence are pursued as measures of success, and leadership is too often defined by how many people follow rather than how faithfully one serves. But in the kingdom of God, leadership looks entirely different. Biblical leadership turns the world's model upside down and redefines greatness through humility, obedience, and service.

From the trembling obedience of Moses before Pharaoh, to David's shepherd-hearted reign over Israel, to Jesus Christ—the perfect example of servant leadership—Scripture reveals that true leadership is rooted not in authority but in surrender. God's leaders are not those who seek recognition, but those who seek righteousness. They are men and women who understand that the power to lead does not come from position, but from God's presence.

This 28-day devotional journey is designed to help you grow in your calling as a leader—whether you lead in your church, your workplace, your community, or your own home. Every believer is called to influence others, and therefore, every believer is called to lead. Each day will present a passage of Scripture from the King James Version, followed by a devotional reflection, a key leadership principle, and a prayer to guide your response.

You will be encouraged to develop character over comfort, to pursue vision with faith, to serve with compassion, and to persevere through challenges with hope. Each devotional is written to help you think deeply, pray earnestly, and live out leadership that reflects the heart of Christ. Take time to pause, meditate, and allow the Holy Spirit to speak to you personally through these pages.

Leadership in God's kingdom is not a title—it is a testimony. It is a daily walk of faith, humility, and courage. As you begin this devotional, open your heart to the refining work of God. Be ready to be challenged, strengthened, and equipped for the path ahead.

The call to lead is not a call to prominence—it is a call to purpose. And like our Savior, we are called not to be served, but to serve. May these next 28 days draw you closer to the heart of the Great Shepherd and empower you to lead others in His way.

Day 1: Called to Lead

Scripture: Exodus 3:10 —

> *"Come now therefore, and I will send thee unto Pharaoh, that thou mayest bring forth my people the children of Israel out of Egypt."*

Devotion:

The call to leadership often comes when we least expect it and, at times, when we feel least prepared. Moses wasn't pursuing leadership or recognition when God called him. After years in Pharaoh's palace, Moses had settled into a quiet, obscure life tending sheep in Midian. It was there—in isolation and humility—that God interrupted his ordinary day with an extraordinary purpose.

When God spoke from the burning bush, Moses faced the weight of divine calling. The task was massive: confront Pharaoh, lead a nation out of slavery, and shepherd them through the wilderness. Moses immediately saw his limitations—his past mistakes, his weaknesses, and his fears. But God reminded him that His call was not about Moses' ability; it was about God's presence and power. "Certainly I will be with thee," God said (Exodus 3:12).

Many of us wrestle with similar doubts. When God calls us to lead—whether at home, at work, or in ministry—we often respond like Moses: "Who am I?" But God's response never changes: "I will be with you." Leadership in God's kingdom doesn't begin with confidence in self but with confidence in Him. The Lord delights in using imperfect vessels to display His perfect power.

If God is calling you to lead in some capacity, don't wait until you feel ready—obedience comes before assurance. Say "yes" even when you don't see how it will all work out. The One who calls you is faithful to equip you.

Leadership Principle: God doesn't call the qualified; He qualifies the called. Your availability matters more than your ability.

Prayer:
Heavenly Father, thank You for calling me even when I feel unworthy or unprepared. Teach me to trust in Your presence more than my own strength. Give me courage to obey Your voice and faith to follow wherever You lead. Use me to lead with humility and purpose for Your glory. Amen.

Reflection Questions:

1. In what areas of your life might God be calling you to lead, even if you don't feel qualified?

   _____

   _____

2. How have your past experiences or insecurities shaped the way you respond to God's calling?

   _____

   _____

3. What would it look like to trust God's presence more than your own preparation or ability this week?

   _____

   _____

Notes

Day 2: The Heart of a Shepherd

Scripture: Psalm 78:72

> *"So he fed them according to the integrity of his heart; and guided them by the skilfulness of his hands."*

Devotion:

David's leadership began not on a throne, but in the pasture. Before he ever wore a crown, he carried a shepherd's staff. God shaped his leadership not through comfort and recognition, but through responsibility and solitude. Watching over sheep taught David how to protect, guide, and care deeply for those under his watch—lessons that would later define his reign as Israel's king.

Psalm 78:72 describes David's leadership with two powerful words: integrity and skillfulness. Integrity speaks to his inner life—the sincerity of his motives, his moral consistency, and his devotion to God. Skillfulness describes his practical competence—the ability to make wise, effective decisions and lead with excellence. One without the other is incomplete.

Some leaders possess great charisma but lack integrity; others have pure motives but lack discipline or vision. But true leadership in God's eyes requires both a heart that is pure and hands that are prepared. David's heart was right before God, and his hands were trained for battle and stewardship.

As leaders, we must continually ask God to refine both areas. Integrity keeps our leadership grounded in righteousness. Skill keeps it fruitful and effective. A shepherd's heart leads people with compassion and truth, always pointing them back to God, the true Shepherd of their souls.

Leadership Principle: Effective leadership combines a heart of integrity with hands of excellence.

Prayer:

Lord, give me a shepherd's heart and skilled hands. Help me to lead with compassion, honesty, and diligence. Teach me to value character above recognition and faithfulness above success. May my leadership reflect Your care and bring glory to Your name. Amen.

Reflection Questions:

1. Do you tend to focus more on developing your leadership skills or your spiritual integrity? Why?

   _____

   _____

2. How can you cultivate both a pure heart and skillful hands in your current leadership role?

   _____

   _____

3. What "sheep" has God entrusted to your care, and how can you lead them with compassion and diligence today?

   _____

   _____

Notes

Day 3: Servant Leadership

Scripture: Matthew 23:11 —

"But he that is greatest among you shall be your servant."

Devotion:

Jesus turned the world's definition of greatness upside down. In His kingdom, leadership is not about status but service. The greatest leader is not the one who demands attention but the one who willingly stoops to wash feet. When Jesus knelt before His disciples with a towel and basin, He gave us a living picture of leadership defined by humility and love.

Servant leadership doesn't mean lack of strength or direction—it means using strength for the benefit of others. Jesus had all authority in heaven and earth, yet He chose to serve. True servant leaders are secure enough to lower themselves because they understand that leadership is stewardship, not ownership.

In every sphere—whether family, ministry, or career—leaders are called to put others first. This means listening before speaking, seeking others' growth before your own gain, and leading with a heart that mirrors Christ's compassion. When people know you genuinely care for them, they will follow your example more than your instructions.

Jesus' model challenges us daily: Are we leading to be seen, or leading to serve? When leadership becomes about titles or control, it loses its power. But when it becomes about service and love, it transforms hearts.

Leadership Principle: Greatness in God's Kingdom is measured by humility and service.

Prayer:
Lord Jesus, thank You for showing us what true leadership looks like. Teach me to lead as You led—with humility, love, and sacrifice. Help me to see leadership not as a right to rule, but as an opportunity to serve. Let my actions reflect Your heart in every decision I make. Amen.

Reflection Questions:

1. When you think about leadership, do you naturally view it as an opportunity to serve or to be recognized?

   _____

   _____

2. What practical ways can you "wash feet" in your home, church, or workplace this week?

   _____

   _____

3. How can you remind yourself daily that true greatness in God's Kingdom comes through humility and service?

   _____

   _____

Notes

Day 4: Leading with Vision

Scripture: Proverbs 29:18 —

> *"Where there is no vision, the people perish: but he that keepeth the law, happy is he."*

Devotion:

Every great move of God begins with vision—an inspired glimpse of what could be when His will is done on earth. Vision gives direction, focus, and hope. Without it, people lose heart and drift aimlessly. A leader without vision is like a ship without a compass—moving, but without purpose.

Godly vision doesn't come from ambition or personal goals; it flows from intimacy with God. Vision is born when we spend time in His Word and seek His will above our own. It aligns our plans with His promises and keeps us steady when circumstances grow uncertain.

When God gives you vision, it will often seem bigger than your ability to achieve. That's intentional. God-sized vision forces dependence on Him. Like Nehemiah rebuilding Jerusalem's walls or Joseph interpreting Pharaoh's dreams, vision from God requires both faith and obedience to bring it to pass.

Leaders are called to communicate vision clearly—to help others see not only what is, but what could be through God's power. When people catch that vision, unity grows, purpose deepens, and faith ignites.

Leadership Principle: Leaders provide vision grounded in God's Word and led by the Spirit.

Prayer:

Father, open my eyes to see beyond what is visible. Give me a vision that reflects Your heart and purposes. Help me lead with clarity, faith, and conviction, and guide others toward Your truth. Let my leadership inspire hope and obedience to You. Amen.

Reflection Questions:

1. What vision has God placed in your heart that requires faith to see fulfilled?

   _____

   _____

2. How much of your current leadership direction is based on your own plans versus God's revealed purpose?

   _____

   _____

3. What steps can you take this week to clarify and communicate God's vision to those you lead?

   _____

   _____

Notes

Day 5: Faith Over Fear

Scripture: 2 Timothy 1:7 —

"For God hath not given us the spirit of fear; but of power, and of love, and of a sound mind."

Devotion:

Fear is one of the greatest enemies of leadership. It whispers that we're not enough, that failure is certain, and that obedience is too costly. Timothy knew that struggle well. As a young leader, he faced opposition and pressure that tempted him to shrink back. Paul's reminder to him is the same reminder for us today: fear is not from God.

God equips His leaders not with fear, but with power, love, and a sound mind. Power gives courage to act when it's uncomfortable. Love compels us to serve others selflessly. A sound mind keeps us grounded in truth rather than emotion. Together, these gifts enable leaders to face challenges with confidence in God's presence.

Fear will always try to paralyze faith. But every time we choose to trust God instead of retreating, we grow stronger. Courage isn't the absence of fear—it's moving forward despite it, knowing who goes before us.

When leaders walk in faith, they inspire others to do the same. Faith is contagious, just as fear is. Let your confidence in God's power create courage in those you lead.

Leadership Principle: Faithful leaders reject fear and trust the power of God's Spirit within them.

Prayer:

God, thank You for giving me power, love, and a sound mind. When fear rises, remind me of Your Spirit within me. Help me to lead boldly and wisely, trusting that You are greater than every challenge I face. Strengthen my faith so that others may find courage through my example. Amen.

Reflection Questions:

1. What specific fears tend to hold you back from leading boldly?

   _____

   _____

2. How can you practically replace fear-filled thoughts with faith-filled truth from Scripture?

   _____

   _____

3. Who in your life needs to see your courage so that their faith might also be strengthened?

   _____

   _____

Notes

Day 6: Leading Through Trials

Scripture: Romans 5:3-4 —

> *"...we glory in tribulations also: knowing that tribulation worketh patience; and patience, experience; and experience, hope."*

Devotion:

Every leader will walk through seasons of hardship. Trials are not a sign of failure but of formation. They are God's training ground for stronger faith, deeper wisdom, and greater influence. Paul teaches that tribulation produces patience, patience shapes character, and character gives birth to hope. This is the refining process of godly leadership.

When challenges come, the world's instinct is to escape them—but godly leaders learn from them. Trials reveal what we truly trust in. They expose weak foundations and deepen dependence on God. Through adversity, God transforms leaders from fragile to faithful.

Consider Joseph's journey from the pit to the palace, or Daniel's faith in the lions' den—both were strengthened through suffering. God uses pressure to purify purpose. Your pain has a purpose too.

If you are in a season of difficulty, hold fast. Don't let discouragement dictate your response. Let endurance mature your faith and point others to Christ, the One who endured the cross for our sake.

Leadership Principle: Trials shape leaders into people of resilience, character, and hope.

Prayer:
Lord, thank You for using trials to strengthen my faith. Help me to lead with patience and perseverance, even when the road is hard. Teach me to trust You more deeply and to see Your purpose in every season. May my response to hardship bring glory to You. Amen.

Reflection Questions:

1. How have past trials shaped your faith and leadership maturity?

   _____

   _____

2. In your current challenges, what lesson might God be trying to teach or refine in you?

   _____

   _____

3. How can you model perseverance for those who are watching your example?

   _____

   _____

Notes

Day 7: Guarding Your Heart

Scripture: Proverbs 4:23 —

"Keep thy heart with all diligence; for out of it are the issues of life."

Devotion:

A leader's greatest asset is not their talent, charisma, or intellect—it is the condition of their heart. Everything a leader says or does flows from it. That's why Scripture warns us to guard it carefully. When the heart becomes cluttered with pride, bitterness, or distraction, leadership loses its clarity and strength.

Guarding your heart requires intentionality. It means choosing what to let in and what to keep out. It's filtering the voices that influence you, setting healthy boundaries, and keeping your spiritual life nourished. Time in God's presence cleanses and centers the heart.

Unchecked, a wounded heart leads to weary leadership. But a heart anchored in God's truth produces wisdom, peace, and discernment. As David prayed, "Create in me a clean heart, O God," we too must invite the Lord to continually renew us from within.

When leaders guard their hearts, they not only protect themselves—they safeguard those they lead. A healthy heart sustains healthy leadership.

Leadership Principle: Healthy leadership flows from a heart fully surrendered to God.

Prayer:

Father, guard my heart from pride, weariness, and compromise. Keep me sensitive to Your Spirit and rooted in Your Word. Purify my motives and renew my love for You daily. Let my leadership overflow from a heart aligned with Yours. Amen.

Reflection Questions:

1. What influences or distractions most often pull your heart away from God?

   _____

   _____

2. How can you create space each day to let God renew and protect your heart?

   _____

   _____

3. What would those you lead notice differently if your leadership flowed from a fully surrendered heart?

   _____

   _____

Notes

Day 8: Leading with Wisdom

Scripture: James 1:5 —

> *"If any of you lack wisdom, let him ask of God, that giveth to all men liberally, and upbraideth not; and it shall be given him."*

Devotion:

Leadership is filled with decisions that affect others. Sometimes the path forward is clear; other times, it's clouded by complexity. That's why leaders must seek wisdom—God's wisdom, not merely human reasoning. James assures us that when we ask in faith, God gives wisdom freely and generously.

Wisdom is more than knowledge—it's the ability to apply truth rightly. It discerns motives, weighs consequences, and aligns decisions with God's will. Solomon understood this when he prayed, "Give Your servant a discerning heart to govern Your people." Godly leaders do the same today, acknowledging their dependence on divine direction.

The wise leader pauses before reacting, listens more than they speak, and measures every choice by the standard of Scripture. This kind of wisdom builds trust and stability among those they lead.

In a world filled with opinions, let God's voice be your loudest guide. Wisdom will not only help you make good decisions—it will keep your leadership anchored in truth.

Leadership Principle: Wise leaders seek God's counsel above human reasoning.

Prayer:

Lord, grant me wisdom from above. Help me to seek Your direction in every decision, big or small. Silence the noise of the world so I may hear Your voice clearly. Teach me to lead with discernment and grace. Amen.

Reflection Questions:

1. When facing important decisions, where do you typically turn first—your instincts, others' opinions, or God's Word?

2. What recent situation revealed your need for more divine wisdom?

3. How can you build a daily rhythm of seeking God's counsel before taking action?

Notes

Day 9: Leadership and Courage

Scripture: Joshua 1:9 —

> *"Have not I commanded thee? Be strong and of a good courage; be not afraid, neither be thou dismayed: for the Lord thy God is with thee whithersoever thou goest."*

Devotion:

When Joshua succeeded Moses, the weight of leadership must have felt overwhelming. He was stepping into shoes too big for any man to fill, charged with leading a nation into an unknown land filled with fortified cities and fierce enemies. God's command was simple but profound: "Be strong and courageous."

Courage is not the absence of fear—it is faith in motion. God didn't tell Joshua to feel brave; He told him to act in confidence because of divine presence. "For the Lord your God is with you." That same promise holds true today.

Every leader faces moments that test their resolve—difficult conversations, uncertain futures, or unpopular decisions. In those moments, remember that courage isn't self-generated. It's the product of God's Spirit within you. His presence transforms hesitation into boldness.

When leaders act in courage, others find strength to follow. One person's obedience can ignite faith in an entire community. Like Joshua, step forward trusting that God has already gone before you.

Leadership Principle: Courageous leadership stands strong by trusting in God's presence.

Prayer:
Father, when fear rises, remind me that You are near. Give me strength to lead boldly and wisdom to act with faith. Help me to be courageous not for my own sake, but for the sake of those You've called me to lead. Amen.

Reflection Questions:

1. What leadership challenge currently requires you to step out in courage rather than comfort?

   _____

   _____

2. How does remembering God's presence change your confidence when facing uncertainty?

   _____

   _____

3. Who in your circle could benefit from your courage right now?

   _____

   _____

Notes

Day 10: Leading with Integrity

Scripture: Proverbs 10:9 —

> *"He that walketh uprightly walketh surely: but he that perverteth his ways shall be known."*

Devotion:

Integrity is the invisible backbone of lasting leadership. It's not merely about avoiding lies or wrongdoing—it's about being a person whose words, motives, and actions consistently align with God's truth. The word "uprightly" in this verse speaks of walking in moral wholeness—nothing hidden, nothing divided. A leader with integrity does not wear different masks for different audiences. Who they are behind closed doors is who they are in the spotlight.

God promises security to those who walk uprightly. When you live with integrity, you don't have to look over your shoulder or worry about being "found out." You walk "surely," with confidence and peace. Those who live deceitfully, however, will eventually be exposed. A lack of integrity might bring short-term success, but it destroys credibility in the long run.

True Christian leadership isn't about popularity or position—it's about trustworthiness. People may not always agree with a leader of integrity, but they will respect and follow them because they know where that leader stands. Integrity creates stability in organizations, homes, and ministries because it reflects the unchanging character of God.

Ask yourself: *Am I the same person when no one is watching?* The measure of your integrity is not what people see, but what God sees. Let your walk match your talk, and your leadership will stand on solid ground.

Leadership Principle: Integrity sustains leadership and earns trust.

Prayer:
Lord, help me walk in integrity. Keep me honest in the small things and faithful in the big ones. Guard my heart from compromise, and let my private life reflect my public message. May my leadership be marked by truth and character that bring You glory. Amen.

Reflection Questions:

1. Are there areas in your life where your private actions don't yet match your public message?

2. How does walking in integrity bring peace and stability to your leadership?

3. What safeguards can you establish to help you remain truthful and transparent?

Notes

DAY 11: LEADING BY EXAMPLE

Scripture: 1 Timothy 4:12 —

> *"...but be thou an example of the believers, in word, in conversation, in charity, in spirit, in faith, in purity."*

Devotion:

Paul's instruction to Timothy is timeless: leadership begins with example. Before a leader can expect others to follow, they must first model what following Christ looks like. Words have power, but example has greater influence. People may forget what you *say*, but they rarely forget what you *do*.

Being an example "in word" challenges us to speak life, encouragement, and truth. "In conversation" means our lifestyle must match our message. "In charity" reminds us to lead with love, not ego or ambition. "In spirit" calls for passion and sincerity that inspire others. "In faith" points to a consistent trust in God, especially when things are uncertain. And "in purity" demands that we lead with moral clarity and integrity in a world that often compromises both.

Christian leadership isn't about perfection—it's about authenticity and consistency. People don't need flawless leaders; they need *faithful* ones. When your team, congregation, or family sees you praying when times are hard, forgiving when you're wronged, and serving when it's inconvenient, they see Christ at work in you.

Let your life be a visible sermon. Every action, reaction, and decision teaches those around you something about your character—and your God. Lead in such a way that if someone were to imitate your life, they would grow closer to Christ.

Leadership Principle: Example is the most powerful form of influence.

Prayer:

God, help my life to be a faithful example. Let my speech, actions, and attitude reflect You in every setting. Shape me into a leader others can follow with confidence, knowing that as they follow me, they're being led closer to You. Amen.

Reflection Questions:

1. What behaviors or attitudes in your daily life most clearly reveal your faith to others?

2. How do you respond when your example falls short of your message?

3. What one area of your life could become a stronger model of Christlike leadership this week?

Notes

Day 12: The Power of Prayer in Leadership

Scripture: Nehemiah 1:4 —

> *"And it came to pass, when I heard these words, that I sat down and wept... and prayed before the God of heaven."*

Devotion:

Nehemiah's story is a masterclass in godly leadership, and it begins—not with strategy or meetings—but with prayer. Before he rebuilt the walls of Jerusalem, he allowed God to rebuild *his heart*. When Nehemiah heard of his people's distress, he didn't rush into action. He sat down, wept, and prayed. That moment of humility shaped every success that followed.

Prayer is not a pause in leadership—it is the power of leadership. Through prayer, Nehemiah received vision, wisdom, courage, and divine favor with the king. When he faced opposition, prayer gave him strength. When the task seemed too great, prayer reminded him that God was greater.

Modern leadership often prioritizes planning and productivity over prayer. Yet a leader who leads without prayer eventually leads without power. Prayer anchors us in God's will, aligns our motives with His, and gives us discernment beyond human understanding. It transforms leadership from self-driven effort to Spirit-led mission.

Make prayer your first instinct, not your last resort. Pray for those you lead, for clarity in decisions, for humility in success, and for perseverance in trials. When prayer becomes your foundation, you will find that your leadership bears fruit that only God can produce.

Leadership Principle: Prayer empowers leaders to act with divine direction.

Prayer:

Father, teach me to lead on my knees. Let prayer be my first response and my constant companion. Guide my decisions, purify my motives, and fill me with Your wisdom and strength. Align my leadership with Your will so that all I do brings glory to Your name. Amen.

Reflection Questions:

1. How often do you invite God into your leadership decisions through prayer before acting?

_____

_____

2. What might change in your ministry or workplace if prayer became your first step instead of your fallback?

_____

_____

3. Who can you intentionally pray for today among those you lead or influence?

_____

_____

Notes

Day 13: Leading with Compassion

Scripture: Matthew 9:36 —

> *"But when he saw the multitudes, he was moved with compassion on them..."*

Devotion:

Jesus' leadership was marked not only by power and authority but by deep compassion. He saw people not as interruptions, but as individuals in need of healing, hope, and truth. When Scripture says He was "moved with compassion," it means His heart was stirred to the point of action. Compassion wasn't just an emotion for Jesus—it was a motivator for ministry.

Leaders today can easily grow hard or detached under the weight of responsibility. Results, deadlines, and expectations can make it tempting to see people as tasks rather than souls. But compassion reminds us why we lead in the first place. True leadership is not about control—it's about care. Compassion allows you to see beyond someone's performance and understand their pain. It gives you the patience to guide, the gentleness to correct, and the wisdom to lift others up when they stumble.

Compassion does not mean overlooking sin or avoiding accountability. It means leading with empathy, remembering that everyone you lead is fighting a battle you may not see. When you lead from a compassionate heart, you reflect the heart of Christ—the Shepherd who leaves the ninety-nine to restore the one.

Ask God to renew your tenderness. A compassionate leader creates an atmosphere of safety and trust, where people can grow, repent, and thrive. As you lead others, let compassion be your first response, not your last resort.

Leadership Principle: Compassion builds connection and inspires trust.

Prayer:

Lord, soften my heart. Let me see people the way You see them. Help me to lead not from frustration or pride, but from love and understanding. Fill me with grace and patience, and let my compassion draw others closer to You. Amen.

Reflection Questions:

1. How do you typically respond to the struggles or failures of those you lead?

2. In what ways can you show genuine care without compromising truth or accountability?

3. Who around you most needs to experience Christ's compassion through your leadership?

Notes

Day 14: Leadership and Accountability

Scripture: Romans 14:12 —

> *"So then every one of us shall give account of himself to God."*

Devotion:

Accountability is a word that makes many leaders uncomfortable, but it's essential for healthy, God-honoring leadership. The truth is, every leader—no matter how high their position—answers to someone. Ultimately, all of us will stand before God and give an account for our actions, motives, and stewardship of the people and opportunities He entrusted to us.

Accountability is not a burden—it's a safeguard. It protects leaders from pride, isolation, and moral failure. When a leader refuses accountability, they place themselves in a dangerous position where correction is resisted and sin can take root. But a leader who embraces accountability walks in humility and growth.

God calls leaders to be transparent, approachable, and teachable. Invite wise, godly people to speak into your life and decisions. Be open to correction, and let Scripture remain your highest standard. True accountability also means being honest with yourself before God—allowing the Holy Spirit to search your heart and reveal anything that needs repentance.

When leaders live accountably, they lead securely. Their integrity strengthens the faith of those who follow. Remember: God measures success not only by what you accomplish, but by *how* and *why* you accomplish it.

Leadership Principle: Accountable leaders remain faithful and grounded.

Prayer:
Lord, help me lead with integrity and accountability. Keep my heart humble and my motives pure. Surround me with wise counsel, and give me the courage to receive correction with grace. Let my leadership reflect honesty, faithfulness, and dependence on You. Amen.

Reflection Questions:

1. Who in your life has permission to speak truth and correction into your leadership?

   _____

   _____

2. What makes it difficult for you to seek accountability or receive feedback?

   _____

   _____

3. How can you cultivate a culture of transparency among the people you lead?

   _____

   _____

Notes

Day 15: Leading with Patience

Scripture: Galatians 6:9 —

> *"And let us not be weary in well doing: for in due season we shall reap, if we faint not."*

Devotion:

Leadership often feels like a long road with unseen progress. There are seasons of waiting, challenges that test endurance, and moments when it seems easier to quit than continue. Yet Paul reminds us that the harvest always comes "in due season"—if we do not give up. Patience, then, is not passive waiting; it's active perseverance rooted in faith.

Patience in leadership means trusting God's timing when your plans stall. It means remaining faithful when results are slow, and kind when people frustrate you. Many leaders fail not because they lack vision, but because they lack endurance. God often uses seasons of delay to refine your character before He expands your influence. What you learn in the waiting will prepare you for the weight of greater responsibility.

Every farmer understands this principle: you cannot rush a harvest. Seeds take time to grow, and so do people, ministries, and organizations. Impatience can lead to burnout or poor decisions made in haste. Patience, however, allows the Spirit to produce maturity, wisdom, and deeper trust in God's process.

As you lead, remember that God's timing is perfect, even when it feels slow. Keep sowing faithfully, even when you don't see fruit yet. The harvest is coming—and when it does, you'll see that every moment of perseverance was worth it.

Leadership Principle: Patient leaders trust the process and persevere through difficulty.

Prayer:
Lord, give me patience when progress is slow. Help me to trust Your timing and stay faithful to the work You've given me. Strengthen my heart to endure trials and to keep sowing in faith, knowing that You will bring the harvest in Your perfect season. Amen.

Reflection Questions:

1. Where in your leadership are you growing weary from waiting?

2. What lessons might God be teaching you through the delays or slow progress?

3. How can you encourage others to stay faithful while trusting God's timing?

Notes

Day 16: Leading with Humility

Scripture: Philippians 2:3 —

"Let nothing be done through strife or vainglory; but in lowliness of mind let each esteem other better than themselves."

Devotion:

Humility is the hidden strength of great leadership. It doesn't mean thinking less of yourself—it means thinking of yourself less. The world often measures leadership by status, power, or recognition, but Scripture defines it by service. Paul reminds us that godly leadership rejects pride and selfish ambition. Instead, it is rooted in a genuine concern for others.

Jesus, the greatest leader of all time, modeled humility perfectly. Though He was the Son of God, He washed His disciples' feet. He led not by demanding honor, but by giving honor. Humility allows leaders to listen, to learn, and to lift others up. It opens the door to collaboration and builds trust, because people follow leaders who put others before themselves.

Humility doesn't weaken authority—it strengthens it. A humble leader acknowledges that every success comes from God and that leadership is a stewardship, not a possession. When leaders lead with humility, they create an atmosphere where others can grow and contribute freely. It turns leadership from a competition into a shared calling.

True humility also welcomes correction. It allows a leader to admit mistakes, seek forgiveness, and continue growing. When a leader is humble, they model Christlike maturity and remind others that leadership is not about being above people—it's about being *among* them, serving faithfully.

Leadership Principle: Humble leadership magnifies Christ and uplifts others.

Prayer:
Lord, rid me of pride and self-promotion. Help me to see those I lead as You see them. Let me serve with a humble spirit, giving You glory for every success. Make me a leader who reflects the humility of Christ in every word, action, and decision. Amen.

Reflection Questions:

1. How do you respond when your ideas or efforts go unnoticed or unappreciated?

2. What does it look like for you to put others first in practical, everyday ways?

3. How does humility invite God's favor and deepen trust with those you lead?

Notes

Day 17: Discernment in Leadership

Scripture: 1 Kings 3:9 —

"Give therefore thy servant an understanding heart to judge thy people, that I may discern between good and bad..."

Devotion:

When Solomon began his reign, he could have asked God for anything—wealth, power, or long life. Instead, he asked for discernment, an "understanding heart" to lead God's people wisely. That request reveals a profound truth: great leaders depend on divine insight, not just human intellect.

Discernment is the ability to see beyond the surface—to recognize truth amid confusion and wisdom amid noise. It's not suspicion or cynicism; it's Spirit-led understanding that helps you make choices aligned with God's will. Every leader faces moments of uncertainty where the right path isn't obvious. In those moments, discernment separates impulse from inspiration.

Without discernment, a leader may make quick decisions that seem right but lead to regret. With discernment, even difficult choices become opportunities to display integrity and wisdom.

Discernment also helps leaders understand people—their motives, needs, and potential. It allows you to lead with clarity and fairness rather than assumption or emotion.

To develop discernment, spend time in God's Word and prayer. The Holy Spirit sharpens spiritual perception as we listen and obey. Wise leaders also seek counsel from others who walk closely with God. Remember: discernment grows in humility and obedience.

When you lead with discernment, you protect the mission, the people, and your testimony. Like Solomon, ask God daily for an understanding heart.

Leadership Principle: Discerning leaders seek understanding before reacting.

Prayer:
Father, give me a discerning heart. Help me see situations and people through Your eyes. Protect me from hasty decisions and wrong motives. Teach me to listen for Your voice and follow Your wisdom in every choice I make. Amen.

Reflection Questions:

1. When was the last time you sensed God's prompting but hesitated to act on it?

   _____

   _____

2. How can you better distinguish between your own desires and the Holy Spirit's direction?

   _____

   _____

3. What role does wise counsel play in your process of making godly decisions?

   _____

   _____

Notes

Day 18: Leading in Love

Scripture: 1 Corinthians 16:14 —

"Let all your things be done with charity."

Devotion:

Love is the heartbeat of Christian leadership. Without love, every action—no matter how impressive—loses its eternal value. Paul's command to the Corinthians is simple but profound: *"Let all that you do be done in love."* Every word, every decision, every correction, and every vision should flow from genuine love for God and others.

Leadership without love becomes cold and controlling. It may produce compliance, but it will never produce true growth. Love, however, builds people up, restores the broken, and strengthens the weary. It is patient when others stumble, gracious when others fail, and courageous when truth must be spoken.

Love in leadership isn't soft or sentimental—it's sacrificial. It means putting others' needs before your own comfort. It means choosing forgiveness over resentment and unity over ego. The best leaders lead from the heart of a servant, not the throne of authority.

When love governs your leadership, everything changes. Communication becomes kinder, correction becomes redemptive, and success becomes about people, not pride. Love creates an environment where trust flourishes and hearts are transformed.

As you lead, remember that love is not just another leadership trait—it's the foundation of them all. Jesus said the world would know His disciples by their love. Let that same love define your leadership.

Leadership Principle: Love is the foundation of Christlike leadership.

Prayer:

Lord, let Your love guide all I do. Fill my heart with compassion, patience, and humility. Help me to lead with kindness and truth, and to reflect Your love in every interaction. Let those I lead see Your heart in mine. Amen.

Reflection Questions:

1. How can you ensure that every decision you make is motivated by love rather than pride or pressure?

2. Who needs to experience unconditional love from you this week?

3. What practical actions demonstrate love to your team, family, or congregation?

Notes

Day 19: Vision and Clarity

Scripture: Habakkuk 2:2 —

"Write the vision, and make it plain upon tables, that he may run that readeth it."

Devotion:

Every great leader must learn to communicate vision clearly. Vision is the God-given picture of what could be and should be, but without clarity, that vision never becomes reality. In Habakkuk 2:2, God gives the prophet a simple instruction—*write it down and make it plain*. In other words, define the vision so clearly that others can run with it.

A clear vision unites people toward a common goal. It gives direction in confusion and motivation in difficulty. When people understand *why* something matters, they will endure almost any *how*. But when vision is vague, confusion replaces commitment, and frustration replaces faith. God calls leaders to articulate purpose with simplicity and conviction.

Spirit-led vision always aligns with Scripture and glorifies God, not self. It's not about personal ambition—it's about divine assignment. As you lead, take time to seek God's heart for the people or mission entrusted to you. Ask: "What is God asking us to build? What values must we protect? What destination are we moving toward?"

Once the vision is clear, repeat it often. A vision cast once is heard; a vision lived out daily is believed. Remember, leadership clarity isn't just about having the right words—it's about living the message you communicate.

Leadership Principle: Clear vision energizes and unites those you lead.

Prayer:
God, give me clarity of vision. Help me to see Your plans with spiritual eyes and communicate them with simplicity and passion. Guard me from distraction and confusion, and help me lead others with purpose and direction that honor You. Amen.

Reflection Questions:

1. How clearly have you communicated God's vision to those you lead?

   _____

   _____

2. What distractions or "extra noise" might be clouding the mission right now?

   _____

   _____

3. What habits could help you stay focused on God's direction rather than your own agenda?

   _____

   _____

NOTES

Day 20: Leading with Endurance

Scripture: Hebrews 12:1 —

"...let us run with patience the race that is set before us."

Devotion:

Leadership is not a sprint—it's a marathon. It requires endurance, persistence, and focus. The writer of Hebrews compares the Christian life to a race that demands patience and perseverance. Every leader will encounter obstacles, discouragement, and seasons where progress feels slow or the finish line seems distant. Yet endurance is what separates those who start strong from those who finish well.

Endurance begins with perspective. The verse reminds us to "lay aside every weight." Some burdens are not sinful, but they slow us down—worry, comparison, or misplaced priorities. A wise leader regularly evaluates what is draining their focus or joy and surrenders it to God.

Endurance also requires rhythm. Even Jesus withdrew to pray, rest, and renew His strength. Leaders who never pause eventually burn out. Spiritual endurance is not powered by sheer willpower—it's sustained by God's grace through daily fellowship with Him.

Finally, endurance keeps its eyes on the right goal. The next verse reminds us to look "unto Jesus, the author and finisher of our faith." When leadership gets hard, fix your focus on Christ. He endured the cross for the joy set before Him. Likewise, your leadership has eternal impact when you endure for the sake of the gospel.

Leadership Principle: Enduring leaders finish well by staying focused on Jesus.

Prayer:

Lord, help me to run with endurance the race You've placed before me. Strengthen me when I grow weary, and teach me to find rest in Your presence. Keep my focus on You so that I may lead faithfully and finish well. Amen.

Reflection Questions:

1. What "weights" or unnecessary burdens are slowing your spiritual and leadership pace?

   _____

   _____

2. How do you currently rest and renew your strength in the midst of responsibility?

   _____

   _____

3. What helps you keep your eyes fixed on Jesus when leadership feels exhausting?

   _____

   _____

Notes

Day 21: Leading in Truth

Scripture: John 8:32 —

> *"And ye shall know the truth, and the truth shall make you free."*

Devotion:

Truth is the foundation of all godly leadership. In a world full of deception and half-truths, leaders who stand firmly on truth become beacons of stability and trust. Jesus declared that truth brings freedom—not just intellectual understanding, but spiritual liberation. When a leader walks in truth, they lead others into that same freedom.

Leading in truth means more than simply avoiding lies. It means embracing honesty in motives, speech, and actions. It's about making decisions that align with biblical principles, even when they are unpopular or costly. A truthful leader doesn't manipulate outcomes or twist facts to look good—they stand firmly on what's right because their ultimate accountability is to God, not man.

Truth also requires courage. The temptation to soften or hide truth to please people is strong, but compromise weakens both message and mission. Truth spoken in love may sting at first, but it always heals in the end. A leader who speaks truth graciously helps others grow and protects the integrity of the community they lead.

When leaders embrace truth, they create cultures of transparency and trust. People can follow confidently, knowing their leader's yes means yes, and their no means no. The truth sets both the leader and their followers free to walk in the light of God's wisdom.

Leadership Principle: Truthful leaders foster trust and inspire righteousness.

Prayer:
Father, help me to love and live the truth. Make me bold enough to speak it and humble enough to receive it. Guard my heart from deception and compromise. Let my leadership be rooted in Your truth and bring freedom to those I lead. Amen.

Reflection Questions:

1. Are there situations where telling the full truth feels difficult or risky?

2. How does your commitment to truth influence the trust of those you lead?

3. How can you speak truth in love so that it builds up rather than tears down?

Notes

Day 22: Leading Through Change

Scripture: Isaiah 43:19 —

"Behold, I will do a new thing; now it shall spring forth; shall ye not know it?"

Devotion:

Change is one of the greatest tests of leadership. It challenges comfort zones, disrupts routines, and forces both leaders and followers to trust in what they cannot yet see. In Isaiah 43:19, God reminds His people that He is always doing something new—something that may not fit the patterns of the past. Spiritual leaders must learn to recognize and cooperate with God's new work rather than resist it.

Change can be unsettling, but it is also a sign of growth. When God brings change, He is not abandoning what was; He is fulfilling what's next. Too often, leaders cling to old methods that once worked, forgetting that the message never changes, but the means often do. God doesn't recycle yesterday's miracles—He creates new ones.

To lead through change, we must first lead with faith. Ask God for discernment to see His hand in the shift. Be willing to release what's familiar to make room for what's fruitful. Communicate the "why" behind the change to those you lead; people can endure uncertainty when they understand the purpose.

Most importantly, don't rush what God is unfolding. Some new things take time to reveal their full beauty. Trust that the same God who begins a new work will also sustain it. When leaders move with God's timing, they guide others from fear to faith, from comfort to calling.

Leadership Principle: Godly leaders embrace change as part of His unfolding purpose.

Prayer:
Lord, help me recognize when You are doing a new thing. Give me courage to release what no longer serves Your plan and faith to follow You into the unknown. Let every change draw me and those I lead closer to Your will. Amen.

Reflection Questions:

1. How do you typically respond when God begins to change familiar circumstances or methods?

2. What new thing might God be trying to do in or through your leadership right now?

3. How can you help others navigate change with faith instead of fear?

Notes

Day 23: Leading with Joy

Scripture: Philippians 4:4 —

"Rejoice in the Lord always: and again I say, Rejoice."

Devotion:

Joy is one of the most underrated strengths of leadership. True joy is not dependent on circumstances—it flows from a heart anchored in Christ. The Apostle Paul wrote these words while imprisoned, yet his letter to the Philippians radiates joy. How is that possible? Because joy is a spiritual choice, not an emotional reaction.

Leaders often face stress, criticism, and fatigue. When joy fades, discouragement takes its place. But joy is what keeps the heart light and the vision bright. It reminds us that our labor in the Lord is not in vain. Joy fuels endurance, creativity, and hope. A joyful leader inspires others far more than a driven one.

To lead with joy, focus on gratitude. Thank God daily for the privilege to lead and serve. Celebrate progress, not just perfection. Learn to see God's hand even in trials—those moments shape character and deepen faith. Surround yourself with people who encourage rather than drain your spirit.

Most importantly, stay connected to the Source of joy. Time in God's presence restores what pressure tries to steal. Psalm 16:11 says, "In Your presence is fullness of joy." The more you abide in Christ, the more His joy flows through you into your leadership.

Leadership Principle: Joyful leaders create hope-filled environments that reflect Christ's heart.

Prayer:
Father, fill my heart with Your joy today. Teach me to lead from a place of gratitude, not frustration. Let my joy be a testimony of Your goodness to everyone I serve. Amen.

Reflection Questions:

1. What circumstances most often rob you of joy in leadership?

   _____

   _____

2. How does gratitude help restore your perspective and enthusiasm?

   _____

   _____

3. What can you intentionally celebrate today to remind yourself—and others—of God's goodness?

   _____

   _____

Notes

Day 24: The Power of Encouragement

Scripture: 1 Thessalonians 5:11 —

"Therefore encourage one another and build each other up, just as in fact you are doing."

Devotion:

Every leader has the power to build or break the spirit of those they lead. Encouragement is one of the simplest yet most powerful tools of leadership. The Apostle Paul repeatedly urged believers to build each other up through words and actions that strengthen faith. Encouragement doesn't just make people feel good—it reminds them that God is at work in their lives.

Leaders who encourage understand that everyone needs affirmation. People are often fighting unseen battles. A word of kindness or recognition can rekindle hope and renew motivation. Encouragement isn't flattery—it's truth spoken to uplift. When a leader acknowledges effort, faithfulness, or growth, it reinforces what is good and godly.

Encouragement also multiplies influence. Teams thrive when their leaders are known for noticing the best in people. It creates trust and loyalty. Even when correction is necessary, it should be balanced with encouragement. Jesus modeled this perfectly—He spoke truth, but He also restored and inspired His followers.

Leaders must first receive encouragement from God's Word to give it to others. Spend time meditating on His promises and let His love fill your heart. From that place, speak life into others. A leader's words can either drain or develop those around them—choose to be a builder.

Leadership Principle: Encouraging leaders strengthen faith and inspire growth in others.

Prayer:

Lord, help me to be a source of encouragement today. Teach me to notice the good in others and to speak words that lift and strengthen. May my leadership bring hope, healing, and renewed faith to those You've placed in my care. Amen.

Reflection Questions:

1. Who in your circle most needs a word of encouragement right now?

   _____

   _____

2. How can you make encouragement a consistent part of your leadership style?

   _____

   _____

3. When was the last time you allowed God's Word to personally refresh your own spirit?

   _____

   _____

Notes

Day 25: Humility in Leadership

Scripture: Philippians 2:3-4 —

> *"Let nothing be done through strife or vainglory; but in lowliness of mind let each esteem other better than themselves. Look not every man on his own things, but every man also on the things of others."*

Devotion:

True Christian leadership begins with humility. In a world that praises self-promotion and recognition, humility stands out as a mark of divine leadership. The Apostle Paul reminds us that leadership is not about being first—it's about putting others first. When leaders value people more than position, they reflect the heart of Christ.

Humility doesn't mean weakness or a lack of confidence. It means strength under control—an awareness that all authority, opportunity, and gifting come from God. The humble leader doesn't have to prove their worth, because they know their identity is secure in Christ. This frees them to serve others without needing constant affirmation.

Pride closes doors; humility opens them. Pride alienates followers; humility attracts them. When leaders are willing to admit mistakes, listen to feedback, and learn from others, they create an atmosphere where people feel safe to grow and contribute. Jesus Himself washed the disciples' feet—the ultimate act of servant leadership—and then said, "I have given you an example that you should do as I have done for you" (John 13:15).

Every day, leaders face opportunities to choose humility over ego. Whether it's giving credit to others, taking responsibility for errors, or serving quietly behind the scenes, humility strengthens influence in ways power never can.

Leadership Principle: Humble leaders earn respect by serving rather than seeking status.

Prayer:

Lord, teach me to walk humbly before You. Remind me that leadership is a privilege, not a right. Help me to see others as You see them, to serve with sincerity, and to lead with a heart like Yours. Amen.

Reflection Questions:

1. How do you react when someone else receives the credit for work you helped accomplish?

   _____

   _____

2. What opportunities do you have this week to serve quietly without recognition?

   _____

   _____

3. How does humility free you to focus on God's glory instead of personal success?

   _____

   _____

Notes

Day 26: The Cost of Leadership

Scripture: Luke 14:27 —

"And whosoever doth not bear his cross, and come after me, cannot be my disciple."

Devotion:

Leadership is a calling that comes with a cost. Jesus never promised that following Him—or leading others in His name—would be easy. He spoke openly about sacrifice, surrender, and carrying one's cross. Every godly leader must count the cost and be willing to pay the price of obedience.

The cost of leadership often shows up in unseen moments: long hours of prayer, difficult decisions, or choosing integrity when compromise would be easier. Sometimes, the cost is relational—standing for truth even when it leads to misunderstanding or criticism. Other times, it's emotional—bearing the weight of responsibility with grace and perseverance.

Yet the reward far outweighs the cost. The cross precedes the crown. Those who lead faithfully will one day hear, "Well done, good and faithful servant." God honors the leader who chooses faithfulness over comfort. The greatest leaders in Scripture—

Moses, David, Paul, and ultimately Jesus—each endured hardship to fulfill their divine purpose.

If leadership ever feels heavy, remember that you do not carry it alone. Jesus, the ultimate Leader, walks beside you. His Spirit strengthens, guides, and renews you daily. The cross is not just a symbol of suffering—it's a reminder that sacrifice produces eternal impact.

Leadership Principle: Great leadership requires great sacrifice, but its rewards are eternal.

Prayer:

Heavenly Father, help me to carry my cross with faith and courage. Strengthen me for the sacrifices leadership demands, and remind me that serving You is worth any cost. May my life and leadership bring glory to Your name. Amen.

Reflection Questions:

1. What personal sacrifices have you already made in order to follow God's call to lead?

   _____

   _____

2. How do you handle the emotional or relational costs that come with obedience?

   _____

   _____

3. In what ways does remembering Jesus' sacrifice strengthen your willingness to endure your own?

   _____

   _____

Notes

Day 27: Finishing Strong

Scripture: 2 Timothy 4:7 —

> *"I have fought the good fight, I have finished the race, I have kept the faith."*

Devotion:

The true measure of leadership is not how you start but how you finish. The Apostle Paul could look back over his life and ministry and declare with confidence that he had fought well, finished faithfully, and kept his trust in God. That's the legacy every Christian leader should aim for—to finish strong in both character and calling.

Finishing strong requires consistency. Many leaders begin with passion but lose focus when challenges arise. The key is daily faithfulness—doing the right things, even when they seem small or unnoticed. Over time, faithfulness compounds into fruitfulness.

It also requires resilience. The journey of leadership will include setbacks, disappointments, and seasons of doubt. But finishing strong means getting up every time you fall and continuing to trust God's plan. Even when results aren't immediate, obedience today prepares you for victory tomorrow.

Finally, finishing strong means keeping the faith. Leadership is ultimately about stewardship—caring for what God has entrusted to you until the very end. When you lead with integrity, love, and perseverance, you leave behind more than achievements—you leave a legacy of faithfulness that inspires others to follow Christ.

Leadership Principle: Leaders who remain faithful to the end leave a lasting legacy of influence.

Prayer:

Lord, help me to lead with endurance and integrity until the very end. Strengthen my faith when I grow weary, and keep my eyes fixed on You. May I finish the race You've called me to run and bring glory to Your name. Amen.

Reflection Questions:

1. What daily habits will help you remain faithful to God's calling until the end?

   _____

   _____

2. Where do you need renewed perseverance to continue the race set before you?

   _____

   _____

3. How would you like those you lead to remember your example when your leadership season concludes?

   _____

   _____

Notes

Day 28: The Legacy of Leadership

Scripture: Psalm 145:4 —

> *"One generation shall praise thy works to another, and shall declare thy mighty acts."*

Devotion:

Leadership doesn't end when your role does—true leadership lives on in the lives of those you've influenced. Every godly leader is called to think generationally, passing on wisdom, faith, and vision to those who come after them. Psalm 145 reminds us that one generation is meant to declare God's greatness to the next. Leadership, at its core, is stewardship of influence for eternal purposes.

Your legacy is not measured by titles, accomplishments, or recognition but by the people you've impacted for Christ. The greatest leaders multiply themselves by investing in others— teaching, mentoring, and empowering them to lead. Jesus modeled this perfectly. He poured His life into twelve disciples, who then changed the world.

Building a legacy requires intentionality. It means taking time to share not only your victories but also your struggles and lessons learned. It means praying for and believing in the potential of others. Legacy-minded leaders focus on what will outlast them—the faith, values, and vision that point people to God.

When your leadership journey ends, may others say that you led with love, truth, and faithfulness. May your influence continue through those you've poured into. That is the kind of legacy that honors God and transforms generations.

Leadership Principle: Great leaders think beyond themselves and invest in the next generation.

Prayer:
Father, help me to lead with eternity in mind. Teach me to invest in others with wisdom and love. May my leadership bring lasting impact that glorifies You and strengthens future generations of believers. Amen.

Reflection Questions:

1. Who are you intentionally mentoring or investing in to carry the vision forward?

   _____

   _____

2. What spiritual truths or values do you most want to pass to the next generation?

   _____

   _____

3. If your leadership ended today, what lasting impact would remain in the lives of those you've served?

   _____

   _____

Notes

Conclusion

As you reach the end of this 28-day journey through biblical leadership, pause to consider all that God has revealed and refined within you. Leadership, in the world's eyes, is often measured by influence, status, and success. But in God's Kingdom, leadership is defined by faithfulness, humility, and obedience. True leaders do not rise by self-promotion—they grow through surrender. They are not shaped by applause, but by the quiet shaping of God's hand in seasons of obscurity, hardship, and service.

The greatest leaders in Scripture—Moses, David, Esther, Paul—did not begin as heroes. They began as servants who answered God's call with trembling hands and willing hearts. Leadership in God's eyes is not about popularity, perfection, or position. It is about purpose, obedience, and service. True leaders are formed in the hidden place of prayer, refined through trials, and strengthened in service to others. They are not motivated by recognition, but by fruitfulness. Their greatest reward is not applause, but knowing they have been faithful to God's purpose.

You have been called to lead. That calling may look different for each of us—whether it unfolds in a boardroom, a pulpit, a classroom, a kitchen, a neighborhood, or within your family.

Regardless of where God has placed you, His standards for leadership remain the same. Lead with humility. Walk in truth. Serve with joy. Love without condition. Stay anchored in Scripture and dependent upon the Holy Spirit. Let your leadership be an overflow of your relationship with God.

Remember, leadership is not a destination you arrive at—it is a lifelong journey of growth, surrender, and trust. There will be seasons of success and seasons of struggle. You will experience moments of joy and moments of discouragement. But the mark of a godly leader is not perfection—it is perseverance. What matters most is not how quickly you progress, but how faithfully you follow. Keep your heart tender before God, your eyes fixed on Jesus, and your hands open to serve.

The same God who called you to lead will sustain you as you lead. You are never alone in this journey. The Good Shepherd, who laid down His life for His sheep, walks beside you every step of the way. His presence will guide you when the path is unclear, His strength will uphold you when you grow weary, and His grace will restore you when you falter.

Let these 28 days not simply mark the end of a devotional, but the beginning of a lifelong pursuit of Spirit-empowered, Christ-centered leadership. May the lessons you've encountered here continue to shape your decisions, your heart, and your legacy.

Final Scripture:

2 Timothy 2:15 — "Study to shew thyself approved unto God, a workman that needeth not to be ashamed, rightly dividing the word of truth."

Final Prayer:

Lord, I thank You for this journey and for every truth You've revealed along the way. Let Your Word take deep root in my heart and bear fruit in my life. Help me not only to be a hearer of Your Word but a doer also. As I lead others, may I first be led by You. Fill me with Your Spirit, strengthen me to endure, and anchor me in Your truth. May my leadership bring honor to Your name and point others to Your glory. In Jesus' name, Amen.

www.ingramcontent.com/pod-product-compliance
Lightning Source LLC
Chambersburg PA
CBHW061232070526
44584CB00030B/4095